# BREAKTHROUGH TO HEALING

from

### Epstein-Barr Virus, Fibromyalgia

and

### Other Chronic Illness

~

*One Woman's Journey*

by

## Marilyn Formella

# Copyright

Copyright © 2018 Marilyn Formella

All rights reserved. No part of this book may be reproduced in any form without permission in writing from the author. Reviewers may quote brief passages in reviews.

ISBN: 978-1-980410-46-1

## DISCLAIMER

No part of this publication may be reproduced or transmitted in any form or by any means, mechanical or electronic, including photocopying or recording, or by any information storage and retrieval system, or transmitted by email without permission in writing by the author.

Neither the author nor the publisher assumes any responsibility for errors, omissions, or contrary interpretations of the subject matter herein. Any perceived slight of any individual or organization is purely unintentional.

Brand and product names are trademarks or registered trademarks of their respective owners.

The information provided in this book is designed to provide helpful information on the subjects discussed. This book is not meant to be used, nor should it be used, to diagnose or treat any medical condition. For diagnosis or treatment of any medical problem, consult your own physician. The publisher and author are not responsible for any specific health or allergy needs that may require medical supervision and are not liable for any damages or negative consequences from any treatment, action, application or preparation, to any person reading or following the information in this book. References are provided for informational purposes only and do not constitute endorsement of any websites or other sources. Readers should be aware that the websites listed in this book may change.

Cover and Interior Design:
Marilyn Formella

Author's Photo Courtesy of:
Nancy Rubly, Portraits on Pilgrim, Brookfield, WI

# Dedication

I dedicate this book to my daughter, Alexis, who has been my rock through 40 years together. I am grateful for your undying support through thick and thin. Even though the difficult times were kept discreet, I cherish our communion with nature as our favorite way to celebrate the victories!

# CONTENTS

Chapter One................................................................................................. 2
Chapter Two................................................................................................. 9
Chapter Three............................................................................................. 17
Chapter Four.............................................................................................. 26
Chapter Five............................................................................................... 30
Chapter Six.................................................................................................37
Chapter Seven............................................................................................ 42
Chapter Eight............................................................................................. 49
Chapter Nine.............................................................................................. 58
Chapter Ten............................................................................................... 64
Chapter Eleven.......................................................................................... 69
Chapter Twelve......................................................................................... 76

# Introduction

*"It is better to know the patient that has the disease than the disease that has the patient."*
*– William Osler*

Many people diagnosed with Epstein-Barr Virus (EBV), Fibromyalgia, and other chronic illnesses suffer needlessly. In the United States, 90% of people are infected with EBV. The Epstein-Barr Virus is classified in the herpes family and is also associated with infectious mononucleosis, some forms of cancer, HIV, and some autoimmune disorders including lupus, rheumatoid arthritis, and multiple sclerosis. More than five million people suffer from Fibromyalgia, which is one of the most common chronic conditions. This condition causes pain and stiffness in the muscles and joints, fatigue, insomnia, and depression. It can begin after some type of stressful event. Other symptoms can include: sensitivity to touch, sensitivity to environmental chemicals, muscle spasms, difficulty concentrating, headaches, and bowel troubles.

Many people diagnosed with these disorders are on disability, which doesn't offer quality of life. They may experience a great deal of frustration with just getting through the day. All they care about is being able to do the things they used to do without pain so they can go shopping, pick up their kids, clean the house, cook dinner, go back to work, or be intimate with their spouse—the things people take for granted.

(The following describes my personal life experiences with both of these disorders.)

As a child, I felt close to God. I attended eight years of Catholic grade school, went to church every day, and was educated by nuns. I was very devout and regularly cleaned the church because "cleanliness is indeed next to Godliness." Sister Teresa was the music teacher and the organist in church. She held me in high esteem as her *star alto*. For a time, I wanted to become a nun as did some of my girlfriends. None of us did.

It was 1971 when I was 18 years old and had my first episode with the Epstein-Barr Virus, also known as infectious mononucleosis. The virus spreads through saliva, which is why some people call it *the kissing disease*. I kissed my first boyfriend back then and wondered if that's when I contracted the virus. I recall my mother being distraught over the length of time I was sick, not having enough strength to get out of bed for weeks! Eventually, I got better and was able to land my first job, move out of the house, and get my first apartment.

In 1979, I started working in the sales profession after I was divorced from my husband. I thoroughly enjoyed the early training from some of the great contemporary business philosophers and sales gurus including: Norman Vincent Peale who wrote *The Power of Positive Thinking*, Dale Carnegie who wrote *How to Win Friends and Influence People*, and Brian Tracy, author of several sales training programs (early *Law of Attraction*).

My sales career involved meeting with business people, solving problems, setting and reaching goals, which took a lot of energy. I sold life insurance to farmers in Southeastern Wisconsin, wholesale silk flowers and plants throughout a seven-state Midwestern territory, employment services, graphic arts and printing, financial services, real estate, computer components, and advertising throughout my sales career.

I held several jobs and alternated between sales and temporary administrative office jobs because of continual episodes with chronic fatigue from the Epstein-Barr Virus. Sometimes, I was *down for the count* for months at a time. My commissions were adequate to live on for a time when I was sick. However, after one particularly bad episode, I lost my home, which was very scary. I felt like I was dying. Applying for Social Security disability crossed my mind, but I didn't want to be labeled as disabled. I mustered up enough energy to get another temporary job and carry on with life. It was a hard road.

The medical community didn't officially diagnose me with Epstein-Barr Virus until the age of 35, right in the middle of another debilitating episode when I worked in the printing industry. The doctor compared it to the flu and suggested I take some time off from work. He told me it was psychosomatic—all in my head. That was in 1988. If I could figure out how to beat this thing, I vowed to help others who also suffer.

You may be able to relate to my situation. The physical, mental, emotional, and resultant financial suffering was devastating. I often worked on commission and there wasn't any insurance to pay the bills when I got sick. Also, the support of the medical community was necessary to get approval for any short-term disability payments. Being out of work so often was extremely frustrating, especially being a single mother with no one else to help out with everyday living expenses.

If there was relief for these disorders, I wouldn't have had to change jobs so often. My foundation would have been more stable. I probably wouldn't have lost my home and my position would be more secure today.

Consider this. If there are 325 million people in the United States and 90% of them have the Epstein-Barr Virus, means 292 million people have the virus lying dormant that could be activated under stressful situations. I could only hope that those who may become afflicted have some form of insurance that will continue to pay their bills, that they could afford to have someone come in to do the household chores and care for their children. Hopefully, they don't lose their jobs.

As a young mother, I focused on prevention and treated myself and my daughter with homeopathy, the system of healthcare from Hippocrates—the first physician who treated the patient and not just the disease. This is the *snake venom theory* or the *law of similars* in which you need a minute amount of the poison to reverse symptoms of the illness. In mathematics, it's the principle of two negatives making a positive. In homeopathy, you tend to identify with one remedy. Mine was Nux Vomica and my daughter's, Belladonna. You take a small amount of the remedy sublingually (under the tongue) every four hours for three days. Being a single Mom, there wasn't a lot of money for health insurance, so we did our best to take care of ourselves.

In addition to homeopathic remedies, we also used herbs for healing. There was always a supply of medicinal herbal teas, essential oils, and natural ointments in the house to treat minor illnesses and wounds. These are the forces of nature I believed were good enough to treat ourselves. I loved to read, so I was mostly self-taught, slowly building a healing library. There was always a subscription to *Prevention*® magazine to learn about how to care for myself and my family. Since the doctor couldn't help at the time, I had to do something.

The hope is for a better system of health care that encompasses more than just the prescription that our current system promotes: eat right, get the right amount of exercise and sleep, and know your health hazards that can include saturated fats, smoking cigarettes, inactivity, etc. I would like to see our health care system transformed to develop a healing approach that includes the interaction among the individual, family, and society, which could significantly reduce the costs of health care. We are individuals, with our own stories and experiences, attitudes, values, and personality traits that affect our states of health.

In our current health care system, doctors have become mechanics fixing broken systems. This is certainly necessary, especially in emergency care. Society's purpose is to progress; however, technological advances focus on the diagnosis of disease rather than a focus on patients. We need to prevent disease rather than just treat it. Just like a home has furniture and appliances, it ought to have a massage table and home health care tools and techniques.

We spend more money on prolonging the last year of life rather than investing in prenatal care, teenage family planning and emotional intelligence education, health exams and immunizations for low income children. We ought to be able to pay for relaxation instruction, lifestyle changes, massage therapy and other preventive measures out of our HSAs (Health Savings Accounts) which is money we've saved. Instead, there are strict rules about what is allowed.

The purpose of this book is to help those who suffer needlessly. Through a series of synchronous events, you will get some tools and techniques to try. You will learn what systems of healing are used by other cultures. You will also learn how to keep a positive attitude on your healing journey, what lifestyle changes may be necessary to maintain your health, and the importance of having a strong immune system to fight disease. You will be challenged to define and develop your own idea of spirituality and get in touch with your divinity to become a confident healer and help yourself and loved ones. You will also learn how to develop your intuition through the power of intention, and finally, how to use energy for your own health and vitality.

This is a true account of my personal healing journey, which belongs to no one but me. Of course, I can't make any predictions that my strategy of healing will work for you too. I encourage you to embark on your own healing journey with courage, a sense of adventure, and experimentation. Please consult with your physician, psychologist, or other health care professionals whenever you are unsure of what techniques or substances could possibly interfere with any conditions you may have, or with any pharmaceutical drug metabolism.

# CHAPTER ONE

## *My Story*

*"The human body has been designed to resist an infinite number of changes and attacks brought about by its environment. The secret of good health lies in successful adjustment to changing stresses on the body."*
~ Harry J. Johnson

I have had 36 years of personal experience with the debilitating effects of Epstein-Barr Virus and Fibromyalgia and have made it my purpose to offer a system of alternative healing to help you. While I have been temporarily disabled on several occasions in my life, lost jobs, income, and my home, I feel grateful that I'm still alive to tell you about it.

Storms appear in our lives at the right time so we can learn lessons. I experienced continual episodes of chronic fatigue from EBV throughout my life, always triggered by stressful situations. A sales career is probably one of the most stressful careers I could have chosen for myself. It may have been meant to be so I could overcome the ill effects of these disorders and share my knowledge with others who suffer.

I spent a good amount of time in the sales profession. I was also a founding member and President of the National Association for Professional Saleswomen—Milwaukee Chapter. This was a non-profit association designed to educate women in professional sales. The position I held selling printing became the job I really loved. It offered me limitless creativity and satisfaction. I sold information packaging before the internet became popular. We were involved in new product promotions like trucks and vehicles, training materials, and exercise programs, now classics in their respective industries. There were many deadlines to meet and a lot of stress. Little did I know my favorite job would be the cause of my experience with fibromyalgia.

This was in the early 1990's, at a time when very toxic chemicals and solvents were used to clean the printing presses. Since then, OSHA has imposed strict environmental laws on the printing industry. OSHA stands for Occupational Safety and Health Administration, a federal agency of the United States that regulates workplace safety and health. Soy-based inks were introduced and the use of solvents banned. I worked in inside sales for five years breathing in toxic fumes, and I am extremely sensitive to environmental toxins like perfumes, air pollution, auto exhaust, and mold.

One day, a saleswoman friend of mine who was a print broker, stopped in at the company with her last printing job. Quite coincidentally, she was making a career change to become a Natural Health Practitioner and Herbalist. She took one look at me and said, "You don't look well." I admitted I didn't feel very well either, and my body ached with the pain of fibromyalgia. I was struggling at the time, dragging myself into work. My friend suggested I stop at her home for an evaluation. After taking her recommended herbal healing regimen, I was back in a good state of health, free of the debilitating pain of fibromyalgia within three months.

While working at the printing company, I would often have lunch at the local natural foods co-op, picking up something healthy to eat from the carry-out. This is probably what kept me in balance while I was being exposed to all the harmful chemicals at work. While waiting in line to check out one day, I spotted a book out of the corner of my eye claiming to cure diseases. I remember thinking that was a pretty bold statement to make about something like disease. I paged through the book while waiting in line and there they were—Epstein-Barr Virus and Fibromyalgia! Could there be a cure for what I suffered from? My heart was beating so fast I bought the book immediately, and anticipated diving into the book that evening.

In yet another synchronous moment, I was in a job interview with a former co-worker for a sales position. I lost a previous job where I sold computer components because IT was so stressful it triggered another bout with Epstein-Barr Virus and the chronic fatigue that always accompanied an episode. My co-worker and I were reminiscing about a favorite boss we both loved dearly who had just passed away. I told him I didn't think I could work in another sales job as I kept experiencing chronic fatigue. I was also getting older.

My friend suggested a natural product that might help me. This product ended up changing my life! I haven't had another episode with EBV and chronic fatigue since. And it's been ten years! My heart was filled with gratitude. I have since told everyone I ran into, who was suffering with any autoimmune disorder, about this product. Many people cried tears of joy at the prospect of something that could possibly help them. Suddenly they had hope.

I always believed I could be healed. I also believed I didn't heal with a couple of products. We are not just a body; we are organic beings with mind and spirit. Belief comes from the mind. Belief in a higher power comes from spirit. There were several other healing modalities that helped strengthen my weakened body, mind, and spirit back to being whole again.

My body was weakened from all the stressful jobs and the harmful chemicals. My mind and emotions were affected by the moments I didn't think I would make it. There was a time when Jesus appeared to me and I was anointed, blessed by spirit after experiencing hurtful moments, when I believed I also mattered. There were also past life experiences that helped me understand lessons I needed to learn in this lifetime. I am now 64 years old and stronger than I have ever been in my entire life.

When I graduated from college with a BA in Business and Management, I took a vow to help others whenever I could. I vowed to help small businesses that may be struggling, and anyone suffering from an autoimmune disorder to offer them knowledge. Many people have been helped and I believe many more will be.

## Client Success Story

The following is a true story about two nurses who healed themselves from fibromyalgia. (The names and places were changed for anonymity.)

Jennifer Carlson, age 35, had been a surgical nurse for five years. She loved her job and the responsibility and satisfaction it brought her as a professional nurse. She was diagnosed with fibromyalgia and it was devastating news to her and her family. Her life as a nurse, mother and wife demanded all of her waking hours. The pain in her joints kept her from living a normal life that should include working, shopping, cooking, taking care of her home, picking up her kids, and having intimate time with her husband, showing her husband and children affection they needed.

Jennifer and Jason Carlson have two children, Emma and Peyton. Jason works in engineering, designing roads and bridges for the City of Los Angeles. Before Jennifer's fibromyalgia diagnosis, they lived in Manhattan Beach in joy and contentment. Now, they had to come up with Plan B. What if Jennifer became so debilitated from this disease that she had to file for long-term disability at 60% of her salary? Where would they be able to afford to live? What schools would the kids attend? Could they possibly afford to have someone to come in and help with household chores and care for kids?

Emma and Peyton are sad and too young to understand fully why Mommy couldn't do the things she used to. Daddy was feeling the strain of filling in for Jennifer's roles in the household. He was exhausted and feeling resentful.

Instead of filing for disability, Jennifer found a desk job working with disability patients on claims for Workman's

Compensation and Social Security. Because of her medical background and knowledge, the employer was willing to work with her. If she was unable to make it into work on a particular day, she could share the responsibilities with Amanda, a single nurse who had also been diagnosed with fibromyalgia.

In yet another synchronous situation, I worked as a temporary employee at this agency. I worked with these two nurses, compiling their medical notes for client claims. Both nurses were ready and willing to try anything to heal from the pain of fibromyalgia. I suggested the same herbal healing regimen I tried which was designed to cleanse the body, strengthen the body, and maintain health.

Both nurses came to the conclusion that the surgical rooms in the hospital always smelled from strong cleaning chemicals used to sterilize the hospital. They likely absorbed these harmful chemicals into their bodies. After taking the herbal cleansing regimen, both women healed and have gone on to work as the nurses they intended to be, rather than having desk jobs.

# CHAPTER TWO

## *The Holistic Framework*

> *"Nature heals and the doctor sends the bill."*
> *- Mark Twain*

I wasn't healed in a vacuum. Not one thing was the magic potion. It took my whole being to be engaged in the process because my symptoms weren't centered on one illness. I had to look at the whole picture. When it comes to health and healing, I believe we need to take a holistic approach to treat not only the symptoms, but also the causes of disease. You will hear me say often that naturopathic medicine, which focuses on the patient, needs to work in complement with allopathic medicine, which focuses on disease.

This book is an account of my healing journey and how I reached my destination—a state of wellness and balance. It's the path I chose, however, I couldn't have been healed without the help of several people including a doctor, a medical researcher and inventor, health research companies, an herbalist, friends, acquaintances, and co-workers. I encourage you to do the same. You are not alone.

The framework I came up with to best describe my journey is the word *holistic*. Society develops healthy individuals when it considers all the parts of self, taking into account the whole person. Health develops from hope, optimism, laughter, self-worth, connectedness, support, commitment, a sense of control, and love. Life is to be enjoyed, whatever path we choose: raising a family, pursuing a career, acquiring friends and lovers, learning what we wish to learn, and going where we wish to go. Life becomes less stressful when our needs are met. Health unfolds as a result of really living our lives. Here's how the word *holistic* is defined in the dictionary:

**Philosophy**
characterized by comprehension of the parts of something as intimately interconnected and explicable only by reference to the whole.

**Medicine**
characterized by the treatment of the whole person, taking into account mental and social factors, rather than just the physical symptoms of a disease.

Following is a description of how I broke the word down into a comprehensive framework for greater understanding:

        H – Health and Herbalism
        O – Optimism
        L – Lifestyle
        I – Immunity
        S – Spirituality
        T – Truth
        I – Intention and Intuition
        C – Channeling Energy

## *Health and Herbalism*

  My journey of healing included the use of herbs and continues to include the use of herbs in my daily life. I drink herbal teas when I have a cold or flu, and to maintain wellness. However, they played a major role in my healing from fibromyalgia.

  There has been a revival of interest in herbal medicine. Westerners are being exposed to Asian and whole plant medicines. We want a gentle, natural approach to healing. It may take a bit longer to heal using herbs but that's what makes them gentle. It took me three months to get my body feeling well again after being exposed to harsh chemicals in my work environment. Harsh chemicals can be inhaled, absorbed into the skin, or ingested otherwise through eating or drinking. Since we are organic beings, harsh chemicals are considered harmful, as foreign invaders. I was treated by a natural health practitioner who worked out of her home. Fifty years ago, most patients were treated in the home. I'd like to see this trend continue. Will we come full circle?

## *Optimism*

I would never have made it on the path to health and healing without optimism. One of the most important concepts I learned in sales training was the power of positive thinking. It sure helped me through constant rejection from the prospects I called on. I always looked at rejection from a positive perspective; it took me one step closer to my next customer. Positive thinking will help you through the pain, difficulty, and struggles you may be experiencing. It is the practical application of faith to overcome defeat. Ask any doctor. A positive attitude has helped many patients survive diseases. It will bring you answers along your path, and great joy when you achieve victory over your circumstances.

# *Lifestyle*

As I learned about health through reading, I came across many books and magazines. I always had a subscription to *Prevention*® magazine and came to realize that prevention of illness is a lifestyle. Awareness of the food I ate and the beverages I drank—what I ingested—became a lifestyle. I was one of the first members of our local natural foods co-op in 1971. I was eighteen years old. Their focus is on getting foods to market that are healthy and clean: organically grown fruits and vegetables, milk free of bovine growth hormone, free range, grass-fed meats and eggs, whole grains, nuts, seeds, and herbs sold in bulk.

I encourage you to get to know your local natural food store. At the co-op in my city, there is a book section to learn from and permanent books in the store to use as references for your purchases. The natural foods co-op movement came into being in the 1970's with growing awareness of the adverse effects of environmental chemicals on our bodies and our health. I encourage you to focus on your own lifestyle and be honest with yourself about how it affects your health.

## *Immunity*

    The dictionary defines immunity as the ability of an organism to resist a particular infection or toxin by the action of specific antibodies. Immunity is one of the most important concepts in health and healing. If you have a strong immune system you can fight off just about anything. Thankfully, Western medicine has recently made the shift from Chemotherapy to Immunotherapy to treat some cancers. When our internal environment is too weak to resist or defeat disease on its own, we need to give it a little help. The product suggested by a former co-worker, that was to build my immune system, became integral on my journey to healing. It started working from day one, and I continue to take it ten years later with no side effects.

## *Spirituality*

    It was imperative to include the topic of Spirituality for your healing journey. Spirituality is such a broad concept and leaves room for many individual perspectives. In general, it includes a sense of connection to something bigger than self, and typically involves a search for meaning in life—something that touches us all. Today, some people define themselves as spiritual but not religious and generally believe in the importance of finding one's own individual path to spirituality. I looked at spirituality on my healing path as gaining wisdom. I challenge you to find your own life's meaning and define your own spiritual path.

## *Truth*

We're going on a mission to discover the truth on our healing journeys and I challenge you to face your own truth. When I entered the sales profession, it was at the end of the three-martini lunch era. When society grew to realize that overconsumption of alcohol was probably not good for our health, and more and more people became aware of it, only then did we change. I believe a little indulgence in the things we enjoy can be healthy; too much, and it becomes an unhealthy obsession. There are many truths in life and I will touch on those I believe are important.

## *Intention and Intuition*

Deepak Chopra is one of my favorite authors. I met him through the *Science of Mind* church I attended. He is a Western medical doctor and has extensive knowledge of Ayurveda, an East Indian tradition of medicine. He is one of the people I learned from on my journey of healing, as well as from Wayne

Dyer and Louise Hay. Together, they helped me become more aware of the Power of Intention and the importance of listening to intuition. I will explain why meditation is so important to developing intuition and listening to the "little voice inside" that imparts wisdom on the journey to healing.

# *Channeling Energy*

My intention in this section is to help you connect to energy. I will show you how to channel different types of energy and use them for your health, vitality, and longevity. I will explain how the healing system may be comprehensible in a way that eclipses present day points of reference, for that is what innovations are about: new ways of knowing our position and purpose in the world and in the universe.

# CHAPTER THREE

## *Health and Herbalism*

*"Physicians pour drugs of which they know little, to cure diseases on which they know less, into humans of which they know nothing."*
*– Voltaire*

What does it mean to be healthy? Our Western approach may define health as something like this: body in working order, firing on all cylinders, not sick. Sounds like a mechanic's response repairing broken parts. Doctors have become mechanics, performing operations or prescribing medications to fix us; not something we do for ourselves. We have gone from natural to chemical treatments. Natural plant sources have been put on this earth for multiple uses: culinary, medicinal, spiritual, savory, aromatic herbaceous phytochemicals that have effects on the body.

Don't get me wrong. I have nothing against Western Medicine, as I believe our systems of health and healing need to work in complement. One of my synchronous experiences included promoting wellness around the State of Wisconsin. I felt so much fear from people during the disruptive wellness movement, mostly from the people who sell health insurance. The truth is we worked in complement conducting health screens and sending some people to the hospital when their blood pressure was about to send *them* into cardiac arrest!

My point is that we all need to learn about health and take responsibility for our state of health. Because I was so sick from EBV and fibromyalgia, I read voraciously about health. My unwavering faith kept me going. I was taught never to give up in the sales profession, to be persistent. Belief set into motion the law of attraction. The friend who stopped by the printing company where I worked was studying to become an Herbalist. In my mind, she was there for a reason--to treat me for fibromyalgia and get me back to a state of balance and good health. She was the right person at the right time—an angel.

I went to her home that same evening and she used muscle testing to determine which herbal products in her repertoire would strengthen me. I told her what I recently learned about parasites and she immediately suggested the Chinese Para-Cleanse®, an herbal blend designed to cleanse parasites from the body. The Chinese culture depends extensively on herbal preparations, the intention of which is to restore balance.

There were six gel capsules that had to be taken twice daily, which included: one capsule of *pawpaw* which treats intestinal parasite infections, two capsules of *herbal pumpkin* which supports colon and digestive health, one capsule of *black walnut*, used to treat parasitic worm infections, and two capsules of *artemisia combination – sweet wormwood* and *mug wort*. These herbs contribute to balanced intestinal flora. I took the capsules regularly, without fail, and healed from fibromyalgia in 30 days! The next two months were spent strengthening my weakened organs with vitamin and mineral supplements from Nature's Sunshine®, an herbal supplement company in Lehi, Utah to include:

- *Herbal Calcium* – a blend of alfalfa, horsetail, oat straw, plantain, marshmallow, wheatgrass, and hops
- *Combination Potassium* – a blend of kelp, dulse, alfalfa, horseradish, white cabbage, and horsetail
- *Iron* – a blend of vitamin C, calcium, iron, and phosphorus
- *Defense Maintenance*® – a blend to target the immune system that includes vitamin A, vitamin C, vitamin E,

selenium, barley grass juice powder, asparagus powder, astragalus root, and broccoli powder
- *Vitamin E* with selenium
- *PDA*™ -- a protein digestive aid that includes betaine HCl and pepsin
- *HVS*™ -- a blend of hops, valerian, and skullcap for stress. *Hops* are useful for anxiety, insomnia, restlessness, tension, excitability, ADHD, nervousness and irritability. *Valerian* is an herb most commonly used for insomnia, anxiety, stress, nervousness, ADHD, chronic fatigue, muscle and joint pain. *Skullcap* is used for insomnia, anxiety, and nervous tension.
- *Passion Flower* – an herb used to treat insomnia, gastrointestinal upset, anxiety, nervousness, ADHD, fibromyalgia and pain relief.
- *Caprylic Acid* – a fatty acid that helped treat my candida yeast infection.
- *Astragalus* – an herbal tincture used for the common cold, upper respiratory infections, allergies, fibromyalgia, anemia, HIV/AIDS, chronic fatigue, kidney disease, diabetes, high blood pressure, and to strengthen the immune system.

*Important*: Please consult your physician before using any herbal remedies and make sure they will not interfere with any pharmaceuticals you may be taking.

The trip to the natural foods co-op was another law of attraction moment. My belief that I could be healed lead me to the book entitled, *The Cure for All Diseases,* written by Dr. Hulda Regehr Clark, Ph.D., N.D. She received her doctorate in physiology in 1958 from the University of Minnesota. Dr. Clark performed government-funded research in the U.S., left that assignment, and began private consulting on a full-time basis. Dr. Clark encourages you to *step out of your old world that has kept you a prisoner, try something new, and treat yourself. If what your doctor is doing is not helping you, become a health detective.* Her book has many case histories of diabetes, high blood pressure, seizures, chronic fatigue syndrome, migraines, Alzheimer's, Parkinson's, multiple sclerosis, and others.

Dr. Clark has since passed away, God bless her soul. She conducted independent research, studying all kinds of diseases. Of course, Dr. Clark was a controversial figure. She was arrested in the State of Indiana *for practicing medicine without a license*. The truth is she was a Naturopathic Physician, not an Allopathic Physician. Many peers came to support her and she was released, only to receive an award at the tenth annual forum of the International Association of New Science at Fort Collins,

Colorado. Dr. Clark delivered a speech and conducted a workshop to a standing-room-only crowd. She was given the *New Scientist of the Year Award* in the year 2000.

The author came up with a common denominator for disease—*parasites*. She classified all different kinds of parasites by their individual radio frequencies. Dr. Clark found that parasites can be microscopic as well as airborne. We can breathe them into our lungs and ingest them through food and beverages. I found her research fascinating!

Dr. Clark found a way to kill the parasites in an easy, safe way. She invented a machine called *The Zapper* which killed off all the parasites in the body with an average frequency. For the Epstein-Barr virus, she suggested zapping for 60 minutes (7 minutes on; 20 minutes off; 7 minutes on; 20 minutes off; 7 minutes on = approximately one hour) three times a day for seven days. I remember thinking that was a very small sacrifice to make especially if it was going to rid my body of these harmful organisms. My strategy was to zap the parasites and then cleanse them from my body with the herbal parasite cleanse.

In another synchronous moment, I was chatting with my step mother that evening, telling her what I just learned. She said, "Oh, I have a zapper. You can have it." It was given to her by a cousin who is a Massage Therapist. A zapper is a simple device powered by a 9-volt battery. It's a frequency generator with two copper handholds and wires that connect to a little box with a switch. You wrap a single layer of wet paper towel over the copper to conduct a low voltage of electricity and zap away for the specific times described by Dr. Clark.

The very next day, I started zapping. It's also important to flush the body with water and cranberry juice. I did start to feel better, but not totally healed. After following the herbal regimen and Dr. Clark's theories, my ears became clogged, and I couldn't hear as well. My herbalist friend suggested we do some ear candling, an ancient Egyptian art of vacuuming out the sinus cavity. Being the adventurous one, I agreed to try it. OMG!'

The parasites were going to come out of the body one of four ways: through the skin, the bowel, the urinary tract, or the respiratory system. Since I breathed in all those toxic fumes at work, the parasites had to be vacuumed out of the sinus cavity through my ears! I actually heard them squeal as they were being vacuumed out by the ear candles. Admittedly, this healing modality was rather unpleasant, but very effective. I could hear clearly again and was free of those pesky proliferating parasites.

The two nurses I worked with bought themselves a zapper and took the parasite cleanse. The parasites that came out of Jennifer's body came out through her skin. Her skin flaked for a couple of weeks, and she used a loofah to scrub her skin daily in the shower to keep clean. The parasites that came out of Amanda's body came out of her urinary tract. She called me into the bathroom one day to observe what she passed in the toilet. The parasites looked like tapeworms and were swimming in the water. We were amazed!

If you're planning to treat yourself and your family, I would recommend reading as many books on the subject of self-care as you can. I even treat my pets with essential oils. Cedar oil is my favorite oil intended to keep any fleas off of them. I dilute the essential oil in a carrier oil first, and rub the oil on their paws, their bellies, and along their spines.

While there may be more recent publications on the market, the following books are some that I use in my reference library:

- <u>Natural Healing with Herbs</u>, Santillo, Humbart, BS, MH, 1984
- <u>Nature's Medicines</u>, Maleskey, Gale, and the Editors of Prevention Health Books, 1999
- <u>Everybody's Guide to Homeopathic Medicines</u>, Cummings, Stephen, F.N.P., Ullman, Dana, M.P.H., 1984
- <u>Reference Guide for Essential Oils</u>, Higley, Connie and Alan, 1998-2004

- The Herbal Drugstore, White, Linda, M.D., Foster, Steven, and the staff of Herbs for Health, 2000
- The Healing Herbs, Castleman, Michael, 1991
- The Woman's Book of Healing Herbs, Harrar, Sari, and Altshul O'Donnell, Sara, 1999

# CHAPTER FOUR

## *Optimism*

*"The healing system is the way the body mobilizes all its resources to combat disease. The belief system is often the activator of the healing system."*
– Norman Cousins

I believed I would be healed. I always had faith. There were plenty of negative influences around me to help me give up. I refused to listen to any negative people around me. It took more than mental toughness to get beyond these influences. From my experience with *The Science of Mind*, I learned that thoughts are things; they create our reality. Our thoughts are the result of our beliefs. We need to be extra careful about what we believe and the thoughts we allow into our minds. Thoughts lead to actions. Actions lead to habits. If we want to change our lives, we simply need to change our thoughts.

One of the best influences I ran across along my healing journey was Louise Hay, author of the book, *You Can Heal Your Life*. She escaped an abusive father in Germany, came to the United States with her mother and her sister, became a minister in the *Science of Mind* church, and helped many people along their self-healing journeys. She also founded Hay House Publishing, a new thought and self-help publisher. Louise Hay affirmed, "Everything I need to know is revealed to me." Repeating this affirmation activated the Law of Attraction and manifested the knowledge I needed to heal.

In her book, Louise Hay suggests new thought patterns for many problems, illnesses and disorders. Here's what she says about the Epstein-Barr Virus:

**Probable Cause:** Pushing beyond one's limits. Fear of not being good enough. Draining all inner support. Epstein-Barr Virus is the stress virus.

**New Thought Pattern:** I relax and recognize my self-worth. I am good enough. Life is easy and joyful.

I certainly did push beyond my limits in the sales profession. It was encouraged. There were always lofty goals to meet and monetary rewards that came with achievement. I always had to prove that I was good enough to achieve the goals that were set for me. Think about how this relates to your life. What is expected of you? Are those expectations being imposed upon you by others? Are they stressing you out and draining your energy? What are your expectations of yourself?

When I experienced episodes of Epstein-Barr Virus, I felt strong emotions like fear, sorrow, anger, resentment, and panic. However, I believed that I could exert some control over the course of this disease and kept moving forward. I knew I had to change those thoughts, feelings, and attitudes and turn them toward the positive. Worry and anxiety are the most destructive of all diseases. Don't worry. Have faith. Expect the best and get it. Expect success on your journey.

Louise Hay doesn't have any specific thoughts for fibromyalgia, so I turned to what she said about *parasites*. There are some healers who think fibromyalgia is just a parasite infection.

**Probable Cause**: Giving power to others, letting them take over.

**New Thought Pattern:** I lovingly take back my power and eliminate all interference.

Amazing! The power had been given over to these organisms that had taken over my body. By taking action and eliminating the influence of these harmful organisms, I took back my power.

I visualized myself as being healed. Whenever a negative thought entered my mind, I would deliberately voice a positive affirmation like: "Life is good. I choose health. I choose wellness." Think defeat and you are bound to be defeated. Practice thinking positively; make it a habit. You will develop a strong ability to overcome difficulties.

I tried to get any emotional and psychological conflicts under control. Emotional upheavals drained my energy. I drew energy from my ability to have some control over this illness. I was enthusiastic about my convictions to be well.

There were times when I would lie prone on the living room floor, let go, and give it up to God, knowing I could no longer do this myself. I would repeat this affirmation: "God is with me. God is helping me. I am in God's hands." These beliefs helped me gain self-confidence and induced increased strength to keep moving forward. I pray that you can too.

# CHAPTER FIVE

## *Lifestyle*

*"The secrets of health for both mind and body are not to mourn for the past, not to worry about the future, or not to anticipate troubles, but to live in the present moment wisely and earnestly."*
*~ Siddartha Gautama Buddha*

I had to take a serious look at my lifestyle. I've always enjoyed working and some people have called me a workaholic. As a single Mom, I had to be. I needed the money. It takes money to live. There's the roof over your head, food for nourishment, utility bills, clothing, and whatever else may be in the budget. I was seeking something more meaningful, beyond the practical.

    My life as a saleswoman took me to places I'd never been…New York City, Atlanta, Las Vegas, Chicago, San Francisco, Detroit, Boston, and many smaller cities in between. It was all very exciting, or so I thought. It was burning me out.

All the travel, rich food and wine, entertaining clients was making me sick. I had to slow down and take some healing time, as I had another episode of Epstein-Barr, and it took months to get back to work again.

Here's where I had to look at my lifestyle holistically, taking into account mind, body, and spirit. I felt a little lost. One fine Sunday morning, I wandered into the *Science of Mind* church. It was a gathering of like-minded souls. The church didn't have a permanent building. We met at Renaissance Place, Vogel Hall, and the Humphrey Masonic Temple, all very beautiful buildings.

It was a wonderful experience. I even got to sing in a concert hall—one of my dreams fulfilled. It was the gateway to becoming a more conscious human being. I started to ask:

- Who are you?
- Why are you here?
- What do you really want?
- How can you best serve?

I started reading *The Science of Mind* by Ernest Holmes—the philosophy behind the church. Holmes explained how we can actively engage our mind in creating change throughout our lives. I felt this was another synchronous event on my healing journey—to be in a state of allowing.

I think we all reach a point in our lives when we start to question the meaning of life. What does it mean to live consciously? I started to focus on what I was feeding my body again, to eat clean organic food, drink pure water and herbal teas, exercise regularly, and meditate daily. Good health is a lifestyle regimen. I was reminded that being grateful for what I have would activate the *Law of Attraction.*

I've dated on and off throughout my life and had wonderful experiences with really great people. One person I attracted was an educational psychologist. I learned so much from him. In one auspicious weekend, we attended a retreat in Chicago with Master Mantak Chia, Taoist Master. At this weekend retreat we practiced channeling energy—Universal Energy, Cosmic Energy, and Earth Energy. We also learned how to cultivate Sexual Energy to use for our health, vitality, and longevity. It was a fascinating practice and part of Chi Gong, the art and science of Chinese energy healing.

My psychologist friend taught me how to live in the present moment. Focusing on the past or the future would put me out of balance. That Sunday evening, when we returned from Chicago, my friend broke up with me. He was dating another psychologist and wanted to move on. I understood they may have more in common. Besides, I was getting really good at letting go and moving on. I was an energetic, creative saleswoman designing information packaging and introducing new products. I was really tired from all the energy work we did over the weekend, so I went into the house and fell asleep on the living room couch.

Around midnight, I woke up, decided to get into my pajamas and sleep in my bed. I was in that half-state of sleep when I sensed a spirit entity enter my room. The spirit walked around the bed, back again, and spoke to me. It was an androgynous voice. I was more tired than afraid. The spirit said, "I understand the stresses of the artist." At that moment, I felt a slight pressure all over my body, and fell into a peaceful, deep sleep.

When I told this story to my brother, who is a minister, he wept. When I asked him why he was crying he said they were tears of joy for me. He described that experience as my spiritual anointing, and that no harm would ever come to me. Again, my heart was filled with gratitude. I knew my strong faith would carry me through life.

At that point in my life, I decided to go back to college. I was 38 years old at the time. I had to work to earn a living, so I decided on a unique weekend program at Alverno College—a women's liberal arts college. I heard so many good things about Alverno that I decided to go for it. Besides, I was an honor student in high school and always wanted to go to college. I was more than ready.

My college experience was the richest experience I've ever had in life. The instructors at Alverno put us through our paces and challenged us to our limits. I was introduced to their balance wheel, which was made up of seven vital areas of life including: health, financial, intellectual, social, work, spiritual, and recreation. Practically speaking, I learned the importance of living with balance. I am aware of fulfilling all these sectors; however, being in balance can mean different things to different people. To me, it means living with peace and harmony every day, having a sense of being whole, and maintaining quality of life.

During one semester, we had to write a global protocol for the uses of the human genome information. The world of science was about to complete mapping the human genome. This hit real close to home. There is a genetic condition running through my family called *monilethrix*. I have inherited the gene and so has my daughter. My father and paternal grandmother inherited the gene, in addition to siblings, aunts, uncles, and cousins.

The gene has been identified as KRT81, KRT83, or KRT86 and they affect the production of keratin, a protein that makes up the hair, skin, and nails. The entire protective hair follicle is not fully developed. My hair and fingernails are brittle and weak. I learned from a massage therapist that keratin is also a key component of the skin that creates a moisture barrier to keep out potentially harmful invaders from entering the body. This moisture barrier also acts as a thermostat for the body. No wonder I had such a horrible experience with toxic chemicals at work. And no wonder I feel so uncomfortable in extremes of heat and cold. I run for the air conditioning in the summer, and for the heat in winter.

I have worn wigs and fake nails, just to appear normal. I work in the business world and feel it's necessary to appear professionally. As a child, I experienced a lot of teasing and bullying because of this condition. Unfortunately, the bullying didn't stop in childhood. Another area of health care is psychological health. The current system of health care will not cover the costs that are associated with this condition. There are many others who also suffer from psychological pain. My heart goes out to you.

Having to write the paper about the human genome was extremely personal and stressful for me. It triggered yet another episode of the Epstein-Barr Virus, so I took the next semester off to rest. It was a moment of awareness for me, however, to realize how important it is to know the physical and psychological constitution of the individual who suffers from disease. I was becoming enlightened.

Deepak Chopra says to become enlightened beings, we move from egocentric energy (focus on position and possessions) to conscious energy, expressing our full creative potential, and hence, changing our chemistry and physiology. I made the effort to live a more conscious lifestyle. I had to make some difficult decisions to let go of things and people that no longer served my best interests. It wasn't easy, but necessary. My lifestyle started to include *living in the moment*. I found that living consciously in the moment reduced my stress level, which could prevent another episode of the Epstein-Barr Virus.

# CHAPTER SIX

## *Immunity*

*"Research has shown that a simple act of kindness directed toward another improves the functioning of the immune system and stimulates the production of serotonin in both the recipient of the kindness as well as the extender of the kindness."*
~Wayne Dyer

E ating a healthy, natural foods diet kept me alive. At least I wasn't adding to the toxicity from breathing in the environmental chemicals by eating processed junk food and drinking soda. Just getting outside in the fresh air for lunch every day helped me stay in balance. These were acts of kindness toward myself.

When I went to see my herbalist friend, she offered me natural herbs from Nature's Sunshine®, a 45-year old herbal supplement company in Lehi, Utah. The herbs were easy to take, in capsule form, designed to cleanse the body from toxic overload, and to strengthen all systems of the body: Intestinal, Respiratory, Glandular, Immune, Nervous, Circulatory, Digestive, Urinary, and Structural.

   I also suffered from Candida Albicans, which is a yeast-like fungus that inhabits the gastrointestinal tract and can cause problems with a weakened immune system. We focused on cleansing the gut and balancing with prebiotics and probiotics. To this day, I eat raw onions, fresh bananas, and plain yogurt almost daily to maintain a healthy intestinal tract. We performed muscle testing for each product to see if it would strengthen or weaken me. I did everything I could to get well including drinking tinctures, specifically Astragulus, to stimulate the immune system. I also took Caprylic Acid which has antibacterial, antiviral, and antifungal properties that helped treat the overgrowth of yeast in the intestinal tract.

   The Parasite Cleanse from Nature's Sunshine® helped me heal from fibromyalgia, but I was still having episodes from the Epstein-Barr Virus. I knew my resistance was lowered each time I had an episode because it took me longer and longer to get well. The last time, when I lost my home, I felt like I was at death's door. At that time, I was experimenting with new ways of healing. Jesus even appeared to me. I thought for sure He was coming for me. While he didn't speak, I sensed He showed up to reassure me I was going to be okay.

As I mentioned in Chapter Two–The Holistic Framework, immunity is the ability of an organism to resist a particular infection or toxin by the action of specific antibodies. Most people exposed to the Epstein-Barr Virus have developed antibodies against it. I learned from reading that the immune system is governed by the hypothalamus, a grape-sized gland that is part of the limbic system in the brain. Scientists have implied that the immune system might respond to stress and emotion, to include the nervous system as the messenger. Hence, the mind/body connection and the study of psychoneuroimmunology emerged.

It's important to understand the individual patient's story, lifestyle and personality traits. For example, as a young single Mom I was a Type A personality. We are known for always being in a hurry, impatient, in a struggle against time. Type A's have high expectations of ourselves and others. These behavior traits make us more susceptible to heart disease and a compromised immune system, because of the continual stress we put on ourselves. I was a perfect candidate for the sales profession.

I was consistently one of the top performers at work. I received an Addie Award in the advertising industry and became a member of the General's Club in the employment industry. I built territories, helped companies install new systems, but was left looking for another job when the companies were sold. I brought in top accounts and doubled a small company's sales in five years. It was enough to stress anybody out.

It was when I dragged myself to that last sales interview that I found my answer. I spoke from my heart when I told my friend I didn't think I could remain in the sales profession. While we reminisced about our beloved boss who recently passed, he revealed the answer that changed my life. He asked me if I had ever heard of EpiCor®. I read a lot about health and healing topics, and I *had* heard about it, but never followed through. I decided to look into it.

EpiCor® is a product brought to light by health insurance adjusters—the people who price health insurance for companies based on their claims experience. What they found was the employees who made this product, and were exposed to it daily, never had any health claims. EpiCor® was originally developed to keep farm animals healthy and has since been reformulated for human consumption—for adults and children.

Since I am not a medical researcher, I'll leave the biochemical jargon to the experts. All I know is this product not only changed my life, it saved my life! I have not had an episode of chronic fatigue since I started taking it. And, I have been taking it for ten years with no side effects.

In essence, EpiCor® strengthens your mucosal armor, increases natural killer cell activity, increases antioxidant power, and improves gut health. I could feel it working the first day I started taking it. I've learned to listen to my body closely and knew it was working. I hope it works for you too.

# CHAPTER SEVEN

## *Spirituality*

> *"We are not victims of aging, sickness and death. These are part of the scenery, not the seer, who is immune to any form of change. This seer is the spirit, the expression of eternal being."*
> *- Deepak Chopra*

Life is a series of lessons. I set out to find more spiritual meaning with intention. You may or may not be able to grasp or even believe my experience. However, just as my healing journey belongs to me, so does my spiritual journey.

I have a couple of dear friends who are very gifted with psychic abilities, which I'll call the gift of prophecy, or the ability to *see* beyond the physical world. One of these friends is a florist who specializes in funerals. She communicates with those spirits who have passed on and helps the survivors with their bereavement and loss. This is her spiritual purpose.

The other friend was a recognized psychic at the age of four. She could see into the future. Her profession was that of a social worker. She worked in child protective services and had to take children away from severely dysfunctional families. She used her psychic abilities in her job and had to appear in court to testify for the children. This was her spiritual purpose.

I was seeking my spiritual purpose. Was it to be the best saleswoman I could be, helping companies succeed? I wasn't sure, because my career was becoming less fulfilling and too demanding as I was aging. Maybe it was my spiritual purpose for a time. Was I supposed to be contributing something more meaningful? Was I supposed to be doing something else? I started reading books about angels and was instructed to just ask.

After asking, I started having more lucid dreams. One dream in particular was as vivid as if it were yesterday. The dream was set in biblical times. I was sitting at a table outdoors, across from a stout man dressed in a long brown monk's robe with a rope tie—the dress of the day. He said to me, "You're not remembering." I conveyed this dream to yet another friend who held gatherings of The Modern Mystery School in her home. The Modern Mystery School teaches the keys to living an enlightened and empowered life. She brought me to a man who was a spiritual medium. We scheduled a private spiritual channeling session for me to gain greater understanding. During that session, I was told by Archangel Michael that I was Joseph of Arimathea in a past life–a man. This was a bit much for my practical, reasoning side, but I went along with it. After all, I was on a spiritual quest. Of course, I had to research who Joseph of Arimathea was. I wasn't a scholar of biblical history but found it all very fascinating. I started making some interesting connections.

Joseph of Arimathea was a successful businessman who sold herbs. There are several theories about who he was. What was consistent is that he was a member of the Council, or Sanhedrin—a group of Jewish leaders who called for the crucifixion of Jesus. He was a secret follower of Jesus, opposed the decision, and negotiated with Pontius Pilate to take Jesus' body down from the cross, with the assistance of Nicodemus, a Pharisee. Together, they wrapped Jesus' body in strips of fine linen mixed with aloe and myrrh and lay him in a tomb owned by Joseph of Arimathea. Joseph made several voyages to Great Britain to sell herbs and also brought the gospel with him.

Well...could this explain why I healed myself with herbs? Or why Jesus appeared to me in my darkest hour? Did he show me mercy because I showed him mercy? Am I to be a healer in this lifetime and help people down from the crosses they bear? I'm not sure. I've been told by intellectuals that to be wise is to admit you're not sure of anything, and to remain humble. I was in awe!

The spiritual channel was apparently my husband in a past life. Back then, I was a woman. Our last name was Farnsworth, which is a British surname. We came to the United States from Great Britain and apparently lost our fortune in America. This got me thinking about all the gender issues people are struggling with today. If we were men and women in past lives, does gender really matter?

I learned about many spiritual laws, one of which is: *Be willing to give whatever it is you need*. So, if you need love, give love. If you need money, give money. If you need healing, give healing. I needed healing more than anything, so I learned how to be a healer. Is it because I helped others with their healing that I was also healed?

I also learned that we are to keep coming back to this physical world to learn spiritual lessons. There is the law of karma—that whatever you sow, so shall you reap. We are not supposed to interfere in the business of others because they may be living out their karma. For example, if you are being abused in this life, maybe it's because you were abusive to others in a past life, and you need to find out how it feels to experience the same pain you inflicted upon others.

A group of friends used to gather on the first Sunday of the month to perform different types of healing for each other. We would first share a meal. The hostess was a registered nurse and there was a married couple who were preachers, and a woman who was a caregiver for the elderly. Our common denominator was that we were compassionate people who cared about well-being. At one of these Sunday gatherings I was the subject of healing.

In one of my past lives, I was a Native American woman who was from a peaceful tribe in Michigan, possibly Ottawa. Our tribe was harboring a white man who didn't want to go to war—probably the War of 1812. When authorities discovered him, they tossed him in military prison and tortured our tribe. While I was lying on the treatment table, the healers could *see* the tree branch that was placed across my neck to keep me down while I was tortured. They used to dismember the bodies of Native Americans and just toss the body parts into the woods to decompose. This practice was abhorred by the Native Americans who are a very spiritual people.

On another occasion, when I was learning crystal healing, I came face to face with my torturer. He knew it and looked into my eyes with the same horror I must have had in mine back then. His job in this lifetime was to preserve sacred Indian burial grounds by relocating them when they were impacted by development...karmic indeed.

These are just some of the stories and experiences I encountered on my spiritual healing journey. My spiritual channel, and apparent former husband, gave me a gift of the book entitled, *Serving Humanity*, from the writings of Alice Bailey and Tibetan Master, Djwal Kuhl, published in 1972. The decade of the 1960's was an era of profound social change. It's when the natural foods co-op movement began and was the time of many protests for civil rights. All the rock, soul, and folk musicians were the messengers of The New Age. Here is just a brief excerpt from *Serving Humanity* that may inspire you find your own spiritual purpose as we enter The New Age:

> *A belief in human unity must be endorsed ... it must constitute the new foundation for our political, religious, and social reorganization, and must provide the theme for our educational systems ... as long as there are extremes of riches and poverty, men are falling short of their high destiny.*
>
> *... This growing idealism is fighting its way into the forefront of the human consciousness in spite of all separative enmities...They are definite reactions to the human demand—urgent and right—for better*

*conditions, for more light and understanding, for greater cooperation, for security and peace and plenty in the face of terror, fear, and starvation.*

If you want to change the world and make it a better place, heed the call to service.

*"You must not only become receptive to having guidance available to you to manifest your human intentions, but you must be receptive to giving this energy back to the world."*
*~ Wayne Dyer*

# CHAPTER EIGHT

## *Truth*

*"The power of people doing things for themselves is very strong medicine."*
*– Kate Lorig, Nurse*

We're going on a mission to discover the truth. We're going to uncover your truth. If you want to be well, you have to be honest with yourself. I've been a healer for a long time and I'm going to share my top ten truths that make sense to me.

1. We must take responsibility for our own health.
2. Our spines need to be in alignment in order for our energy to flow freely.
3. Drinking pure water and exercising regularly is good for our well-being.
4. If we eat junk food and drink soda all the time we are not going to be healthy.

5. Organic fruits, vegetables, whole grains, nuts, seeds and herbs are good for us.
6. Parasites and pollution have caused human suffering.
7. Overuse of antibiotics will put us out of balance; we need to rebalance intestinal flora with prebiotics and probiotics.
8. Our physicians, dentists, and counselors are to be consulted when necessary.
9. The cost of health care in the United States is out of control.
10. We are the sum of our physical, emotional, mental, and spiritual selves.

If each of us takes responsibility for our health we could build a society that is not only healthy, but whole. Just like my friends gather regularly to do healing work for each other, I believe families, friends, and communities could do the same. I also do massage exchanges with a friend who was a massage therapist so neither of us has to pay.

Some of my clients have back problems, mostly from injuries. It's so important to have your spine in alignment, as the nerves run through the spinal column and can cause all sorts of health problems if your disks are bulging or pinching off the flow of energy through the spine. I've recommended several people go to the chiropractor for spinal care. One client had a skiing injury where she did a complete flip, landing on her shoulder. Eventually, she couldn't work because of the injury. Another client took a misstep off a trolley car and fell on her backpack that held professional camera equipment. They went for years without spinal care. One couldn't lift her arm, and the other couldn't lift her camera. After care, they are both back to normal living without pain and suffering.

Another synchronous experience was working for the Department of Natural Resources (DNR). The purpose of this agency is to protect the public health through monitoring the impacts of development on land, measuring air quality, governing waste landfills, and maintaining water quality. I also worked at a major corporation that built plants on two separate continents to help people in Eastern Europe and India to have potable water that is safe to drink or to use for food preparation, without health risks.

Too many people are not getting enough exercise. In particular, I observe many health care workers who are smokers, drinkers, and overweight. What is wrong with that picture? Granted, health care workers often see the ugly side of life, however, shouldn't health care workers lead by example? If we just look at health and exercise as something good for us, we just might be motivated to consider it as a lifestyle choice. Just the other day, I became engrossed in an interesting cable program and ended up on the elliptical machine for an hour, rather than the usual 30 minutes. I learned that if I get my heart rate up to 155 bpm, I can burn belly fat, so I always make it a point to hit that mark when exercising. I also read that cancer cells cannot thrive in a body filled with oxygen. It doesn't take much to schedule a regular appointment with you, to love yourself, and take care of yourself.

In her book, Dr. Clark warns that some highly processed foods and beverages we ingest may be contaminated with the chemicals used to sanitize equipment in the manufacturing processes. She says our livers are overtaxed and can no longer filter out these toxins, further weakening our immune systems, and causing parasite infections. Also, we know that the additives and preservatives in junk foods are highly addictive, not offering any nutritional value.

Overconsumption of sugar, particularly in drinks, stores as fat. If you take the number of grams of sugar and divide by 4.2 you will come up with the number of teaspoons of sugar in that product. A healthy daily dose of sugar is 6 teaspoons. Most Americans are ingesting 22 teaspoons per day! This is almost four times what is considered healthy and safe. No wonder diabetes is such a problem. In order to be well, we must make a habit of reading labels and be ever mindful of what we eat and drink. I encourage you to seek out natural, organic options for a healthy daily diet.

There is a prevalent use of antibiotics today, especially with children, who tend to eat a lot of sugary foods like cereals. The high sugar intake also proliferates imbalance. When antibiotics are used, they kill off both the bad and good bacteria. The good bacteria need to be replaced with prebiotics and probiotics like eating bananas and plain yogurt or prebiotic and probiotic supplements like acidophilus. I always keep a bottle of acidophilus capsules in my refrigerator when I feel out of balance. Your inner ear will start to ache as a clue that you are out of balance. There is also a liquid form for babies found in most health food stores in the refrigerated section.

As you know, I'm a proponent of natural health care practitioners working in complement with the Western system of healthcare in place today. Now that I am healthier and have a steady job with health benefits, I am surely practicing prevention by visiting the doctor at the wellness center, the dentist, dermatologist, etc. I encourage you to do the same. Herein lies the need for community health care.

Costs of health care are out of control in the United States. Half the time, I can't even get a quote or an estimate like most businesses provide prior to making a purchase. I lived in Germany for a time, which is a Social Democracy. I was provided medical and dental care simply because I was a human being in need of care. And, I was just living there on a visa as an American citizen. That was in 1979, almost 40 years ago!

I encourage you to get involved in the politics of health care. There is a movement toward Universal Single-Payer Health Care which means comprehensive coverage for all Americans. There is another movement called the National Health Freedom Coalition (NHFC) which is a libertarian coalition that opposes regulation of health practices and advocates for increased access to "non-traditional" or alternative health care. This coalition believes *individuals have the right to self-determination in making their own health care choices. However, when health care options are eliminated through restrictive laws and regulations, choices are eliminated and access becomes meaningless.*

One such alternative is my favorite healing modality—crystal healing. I've been a Certified Crystal Healer since 2004. To describe this modality in the simplest way, we are beings made up of physical, emotional, mental and spiritual energy centers. This is a good place to introduce the chakra system. Chakras are energy vortices that we all have. While we have chakra openings all over the body, the major chakras run from the base of the spine to the crown of the head and beyond. What is fascinating is that each chakra relates to a color of the light spectrum: red, orange, yellow, green, light blue, dark blue, and purple. (See following illustration.)

*Crown Chakra* — *Spirituality*

*Third Eye Chakra* — *Awareness*

*Throat Chakra* — *Communication*

*Heart Chakra* — *Love, Healing*

*Solar Plexus Chakra* — *Wisdom, Power*

*Sacral Chakra* — *Sexuality, Creativity*

*Root Chakra* — *Basic Trust*

Sometimes, we experience traumas that can affect us physically through injury, or traumas that affect us emotionally through death, divorce, job loss, abuse, etc. We can also experience mental and spiritual crises. These traumas may cause blockages of energy flow and can result in health problems. It is through healing that makes us whole again. Some cultures consider crystal healing essential to our holistic health and well-being.

I work specifically with the chakras when performing crystal healing. A session usually takes about an hour. Specially-selected stones, that have inherently different frequencies, are placed on the chakras depending on what the client needs. Clear quartz is placed around the body to balance the human energy field. Clear quartz has the same frequency as the human body. There is a hands-on component to the session, feeling for blockages of energy flow. When a blockage is detected, it is simply cleared. These energy blockages and the accompanying traumas are released and the client subsequently reaches a higher state of well-being.

## Client Success Story

A young man in his mid-twenties came to me asking for crystal healing. He had recently been diagnosed with an inoperable brain tumor that showed up on his MRI. He was alone and scared, looking for an alternative solution. I started working on him as I would anyone, starting with the first session—*Initiation*. During his first session, I discovered his polarity was reversed. Normally, energy enters the left side of the body, and flows out the right. His energy was moving in the reverse motion. I used magnetic stones to correct his polarity and researched a special stone for him that dissolves tumors. The stone arrived in the mail from a doctor's collection and was used in the client's second session—*Release*. I also had him sleep with the stone under his pillow until his third session. After his third session—*Integration*, he went for another MRI.

The tumor was no longer detectable. He is fine and healthy to this day, seven years later.

# CHAPTER NINE

## *Intention and Intuition*

*"Only through awareness do you have choice."*
*~ Olivia Hoblitzelle, Mind/Body Medical Institute,*
*New England Deaconess Hospital*

To me, author Wayne Dyer was the best teacher of the Power of Intention. He made his transition in 2015. May his soul rest in peace. The dictionary defines intention as a strong purpose or aim. Carlos Castaneda, another author, says intent is a force in the universe. This force can become powerful when inspired, so we may experience life in new and exciting ways, and synchronistic results will begin to happen. This is what happened to me in my quest for answers on my healing journey.

As a Type A personality, I had a lot of impatience, nervous tension, and stress. I also have ADHD (Attention Deficit Hyperactivity Disorder). I've learned the ADHD brain is different from the "normal" brain. Scientific brain studies are just now being conducted to understand these differences more fully. However, I knew I had to go deeply into myself to move from confusion to happiness. I learned how to meditate. Through meditation, I was able to create inner calm, curb anxiety, gain awareness and control, and manage stress. I practiced meditation 20 minutes in the morning when I first arose, and 20 minutes before retiring. Through meditation, I reduced my blood pressure, heart rate, breathing rate, and muscular tension, restoring relaxation. It was difficult to eliminate thoughts when they arose because I was always thinking.

Aside from the physical benefits of practicing meditation, insights were revealed to me. Answers came through my intuition. When on my spiritual quest, the spiritual channel taught me to pay attention to that little voice inside. That was the voice of Spirit trying to offer guidance. I needed to listen more closely.

I had to start with body awareness, particularly the breath. Attention was given to how my body was affected with each and every breath. Sounds, thoughts, moods, and body sensations bubbled up to the surface. Every time I meditated, the stress and tension left my body with every breath. I started to pay closer attention. How did I feel that day? What were my body sensations? Was my body tired? Did I need care? Did I need rest? Was I restless? Was I feeling angry, worried, sad, loving?

Letting these feelings bubble up meant some emotion wanted to be felt. I released these things and brought awareness back to my breathing. Awareness of the breath was training for living in the present moment. My mind wandered to the past or to the future a thousand times, however, I would begin again. My body began to open. I found the place of rest, inner freedom, and peace.

Then my heart began to open. I learned forgiveness. I learned to forgive myself and others. I met awareness with balance and wisdom. I had choice. I chose to let go of the past. I didn't want to carry the hatreds of the past. It poisoned me. I found forgiveness included grief and sorrow. I knew it was time to let go. Each and every day, I practiced forgiveness, compassion, and loving kindness for myself, my loved ones, and all beings in the world. During my meditations, I asked for forgiveness and forgave. Now that I was more aware, I could avoid repeating past mistakes, create and heal through relationships with myself and others.

I practiced loving kindness. It is the intention of the heart to be loving and kind toward ourselves and others. My heart opened. There is a place in all of us that wants to love and respect ourselves and others. Negative emotions arose during meditation. I learned to be loving and kind for those emotions too. I knew my intentions and thoughts had power. I wanted to have a peaceful heart.

I knew I had to change any negative thoughts and express myself through the seven faces of intention which are:

1. Creativity
2. Love
3. Kindness
4. Beauty
5. Expansion
6. Abundance
7. Receptivity

These high energy attitudes are the power behind intention. The power of intention involved staying on the side of infinite possibilities. I have always been a possibility thinker and that is why I was healed. I believed it was possible.

Just as *holistic* is the framework for this book, I had to think holistically about my well-being, which included:

- showing respect for myself, others, and all of life
- forgiving any adversaries, and asking for forgiveness
- being in a state of gratitude, and
- living life on purpose.

I learned my purpose was not so much about what I did, but how I felt. I wanted to feel good, so I had to be aware of thinking good-feeling thoughts. I wanted to feel love, enthusiasm, and joy. Negative thoughts like sadness, depression, and anxiety would only attract more of those low energy emotions.

I believed when I was inspired by a great purpose, everything would work for me. That is why the right people showed up for me in divine order at just the right time. I was patient. I knew I was here on purpose. I had faith in the call I was hearing from the center of my being. I asked myself, "How can I serve?" I meditated to stay on purpose. I had to keep my thoughts and feelings in harmony with my actions, leaving ego behind.

I had to put my attention on what I intended to manifest rather than on the low energies that I encountered. I knew I had to heal in order to be healed. In closing, I want to share the affirmations from Wayne Dyer that kept me focused on the power of intention in my life.

- I express myself through the seven faces of intention: creativity, kindness, love, beauty, expansion, abundance, receptivity.
- I attract success and abundance into my life because that is who I am.
- I know the right people will show up in divine order at the right time.
- Infinite patience produces immediate results.
- I practice being in silence and meditation.

- I am whole and perfect as I was created.
- I am in the state of allowing.
- I am what it is I am seeking.
- I attract peace into my life.
- I believe in my worthiness.
- I am grateful for all I have.
- I believe in my abilities.
- I am ready and willing.
- My natural state is joy.

Repeat these affirmations out loud every day and take note of how your life changes.

*"Change the way you look at things, and the things you look at change."*
*~Wayne Dyer*

# CHAPTER TEN

## *Channeling Energy*

*"Instead of conventional drug and surgical approaches, vibrational medicine attempts to treat people with pure energy."*
~ *Richard Gerber, M.D.*

Through Taoist Master, Mantak Chia, I learned how to channel three different types of energy: Universal Energy, Cosmic Energy, and Earth Energy, all with the intention of using these energies for health, vitality, and longevity. I also learned how to cultivate sexual energy with the same intention. These practices are part of Chi Gong, the Art and Science of Chinese Energy Healing. I use these techniques in meditation sessions and when I conduct crystal healing sessions. Channeling energy is like an incredible power booster to the body—an unlimited source of energy that is circulated through the acupuncture meridians. Allow me to explain.

I attended Chia's weekend retreat in Chicago. Throughout the weekend we practiced meditating under the guidance of his disciples while channeling these different types of energy. In a previous chapter, I described how I was spiritually anointed the evening I returned from this weekend. It was one of the most memorable events of my life. What I learned has become a significant practice in all my healing sessions ever since.

The Taoists have discovered the universe within, the microcosm, and has found it to be identical to the outer universe, the macrocosm. That inner universe is a flow of energy, or chi, that connects three bodies (physical, soul, and spirit). This energy runs up the spine and down the front of the body—a sort of inner alchemy that controls the life force.

Universal energy, or heavenly energy, is made up of the energy from the stars, planets, and galaxies that nourishes the mind, soul, and spirit of each individual. The Taoists believe Cosmic energy, or particle energy, nourishes our organs, glands, and senses. The third force of nature is Earth energy that includes the energy of plants, animals and water.

Using the power of the mind, these energies are absorbed into the body with a spiral motion through different energy openings, or chakras, on our bodies and circulated through the microcosmic orbit, or internal universe. This process of circulating these energies is intended to purify the body and to improve vitality and longevity. I typically absorb universal energy through the crown chakra, cosmic energy through the third eye, and earth energy through the bottoms of the feet and the palms of the hands.

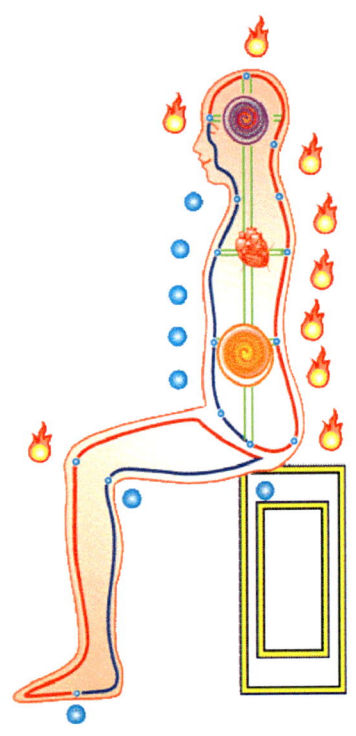

Toward the end of our weekend retreat, Master Chia made an appearance to conduct a guided meditation with us. He guided us through a twenty-minute earth energy meditation and directed us to keep our eyes closed until the end of the 20 minutes. When one of his disciples touched us on the shoulder, we were to open our eyes and look him in the eye. He sat in the front of the room on a chair facing the group.

We sat on the edge of a chair, with our palms turned downward toward the earth. There was a feeling of suction in the palms of the hands, absorbing the earth's energy. We then circulated that energy through the microcosmic orbit, or internal universe, for 20 minutes. Eventually, I could see the shape of my head in blueness—the color of the earth. My eyeballs started to vibrate in their sockets with an energy so forceful, they felt as if they were going to pop out of my head!

I was the first person in the first row, and the disciple touched me on the shoulder at the end of the 20-minute meditation. I opened my eyes and looked the Master in the eye. The energy was so strong and forceful that he practically fell off his chair! He looked at me with wide-eyed surprise and then moved on to the next person. One of the attendees made it a point to talk to me about this experience at the end of the retreat. He said he thought I may have been the master's teacher in a past life. I was in awe of the power of these meditations and I have used these energy techniques ever since.

In a previous chapter, I mentioned taking up the study of crystal healing, which has become my favorite healing modality, as I have seen miracles happen for clients, relieving them of suffering. I use rocks, minerals, gems, and crystals—gifts from the Earth. Crystal healing is a form of vibrational medicine, which is more of an Einsteinian model as opposed to the Newtonian mechanistic viewpoint. Crystal healing works through the chakras and the layers of the human energy field taking into account the physical, emotional, mental, and spiritual parts of ourselves.

Humans are beings of vibrational energy. Crystal healing considers the spirit as it relates to the physical body. It is the energy of spirit that animates the physical framework. The unseen connection between the physical body and the forces of spirit holds the key to understanding the inner relationship between matter and energy. Consciousness itself is a kind of energy that is related to the physical body and participates in the creation of either health or illness.

# CHAPTER ELEVEN

## *Obstacles to Healing*

*"Do you want to be well?"*
*~Jesus of Nazareth*

When Jesus was about to heal someone, he would ask the individual, "Do you want to be well?" Herein lies the power of intention. I definitely wanted to be well, and I believed I could be healed. I couldn't wallow in negative beliefs or victimhood. I had to be optimistic and think positively. I believed I would be healed in time. Whenever I had a possible answer, I was willing to try it. This required persistence, personal resolve and a burning desire to be well.

When I conducted healings for others, I helped them identify obstacles to healing and addressed those issues. Some people wanted to be well and some didn't. Of course, I only had so much time, and worked only with those people who were in a state of allowing. As a healer, I can only jump-start the process. You have to follow through.

Following are some common psychological reasons why people don't want to be well:

- *No Self Love* – Not taking good care of self
- *A Closed Heart* – Building up walls of resistance
- *Negative Beliefs* – Believing a disease is incurable
- *Lack of Forgiveness* – Holding grudges against anyone who has ever hurt you
- *Playing the Victim* – Nothing can be done to improve the situation
- *Doubt* – Lacking faith
- *Need for Attention/Sympathy* – Giving away your power to act on your own behalf and create your own reality
- *Lack of Responsibility* – You've got to do your share or you won't heal
- *Lack of Resolve/Inertia* – Giving up; doing nothing
- *Entropy* – Believing our bodies just break down and deteriorate
- *Guilt* – It's your fault you're sick
- *Self-Punishment* – Believing you need to suffer because you did something bad
- *Martyrdom* – Taking on the suffering of humanity

- *Ego—* Healing won't work for me because I'm special/unique

When people don't want to be well, I recommend they seek counseling to identify the reasons why they are "led to water and don't want to drink." Just as I would recommend a doctor or a chiropractor, I would recommend a psychologist or a counselor. We all need to take responsibility for our own healing and seek out the appropriate healer. It takes courage to heal.

Along my personal healing journey, I was able to identify obstacles that could have easily held me back. I mentioned earlier that I was born with a genetic condition and was the object of bullying. I learned that bullies are not well themselves and they are just looking for someone they perceive to be weak who they can pick on and blame for their own shortcomings, wrongdoings, or to hide their own families' dysfunctions.

I gave birth to one child who inherited this gene, and we almost didn't make it. When I was only six weeks pregnant, I was hemorrhaging, with doctor's orders to remain flat on my back until the bleeding stopped. My ability to carry to term was in question. My daughter was ultimately born with the gene. I wanted more children, however, didn't want to give birth to any more children who would have to endure this same condition and the bullying. It was too painful. I could have held on to these resentments, however, I learned to fogive the bullies, some of whom are my own family members.

Ninety-five percent of families are dysfunctional, so none of us are alone. We have to care for each other and recognize when and where healing is needed. My family suffers from alcoholism, addiction, a genetic condition, and ADHD. Some researchers today are suspecting that ADHD may be the result of fetal alcohol syndrome. Thankfully, I learned the lessons from the overconsumption of alcohol and addiction in my twenties. Through awareness, I was able to make healthier choices. Today, I am a social drinker and enjoy a glass of wine or beer on occasion...usually to celebrate something or someone. Even Jesus made water into wine for the wedding celebration.

I went to ACOA (adult children of alcoholics) counseling when I was in my thirties. I had to heal from an abusive, alcoholic family who lacked personal awareness. I was also mocked for doing so. At the time, I thought this behavior exhibited an insensitive disrespect for my feelings. I was chosen as the family scapegoat. I was the sensitive, sickly one, who was perceived to be weak and could be blamed for all the family ills. I struggled with low self- esteem and lack of self-worth because of it, feeling unsafe and unloved. I am also the outspoken one who refuses to remain silent in the unbearable atmosphere. I came to realize my sensitivity was *the wound that became the gift*. I use my acute sensitivity to this day in my healing work.

I had a marriage that turned bad, and other attempts at relationships that didn't work out. Apparently, scapegoats continually attract people who treat them badly because that is what is familiar. I sincerely thought they were interested in pursuing a long-term relationship with me, when all they wanted was to use me. I was naïve. My heart became closed, as I didn't want to be hurt anymore. I had to separate myself from things and people who no longer served my best interests. It was difficult, but necessary in order to heal. We all have broken hearts for one reason or another. Re-opening people's hearts became one of my main goals in crystal healing.

My lifestyle in the sales profession required that I travel a lot and *wine & dine* clients. After five years, I became burned out. More obstacles to healing had to be overcome. I left more than one job because of what was required. I felt a bit malnourished in mind, body, and spirit. I had to nurture my inner child...that little person inside that needed healthy food, proper rest, genuine caring, self-respect, and love. No one will do this for you. You must take responsibility for your own healing and love yourself.

I've had several encounters with corruption in the business world. Some days, I felt my sales efforts were exercises in futility. I was often discouraged, especially when financial reports were published. I questioned whether the figures were accurate. Moral courage and ethical leadership are what is needed today more than ever for all of us to heal from more than just physical ailments.

It's been a long journey on the road to healing and it has taken a great deal of courage to *care-front* my own obstacles. I will probably never be *fixed*. I am a member of the human race that is imperfect and flawed. I am aware, however, and have opened myself up to healthier choices.

For me, this was a difficult chapter to put into words. The obstacles I encountered were way to close to home. I love my family, friends, and colleagues, and with all respect, I will continue to show them loving kindness. I have forgiven them and hope they can forgive me for being outspoken. I had to put the *self* in *self-respect*. I didn't want to make the opinions of others more important than my own opinion of myself.

Are you able to identify any obstacles to your own healing? Do you have the courage to confront them? Are you willing to follow through and take responsibility for your own healing, be it physical, mental, emotional, or spiritual? *Do you want to be well?*

*As I began to love myself
I freed myself of anything
That is no good for my health—
Food, people, things, situations,
And everything that drew me down
And away from myself.
At first, I called this attitude
A healthy egoism.
Today, I know it is
Love of oneself.*

*~ Charlie Chaplin, 1959*

# CHAPTER TWELVE

## *Are You Ready?*

*"No one can ask another to be healed. But he can let himself be healed, and thus offer the other what he has received. Who can bestow upon another what he does not have? And who can share what he denies himself?"*
~ *A Course in Miracles*

My goal with this book has been to offer what I have received and help you to experience your own breakthrough to healing. I'd be willing to help you:

1. Understand your problem
2. Have a solution
3. Be present for you through your challenge
4. Bring out the truth
5. Celebrate your successes
6. Help you get to the next leg on your journey

You may live with terrible pain and have a deep longing to be free. As a healer, I am willing to help you reach into these painful areas to reawaken hope. My work as a healer is an act of love to help you towards health and wholeness. However, you must be ready to heal and be in a state of allowing or your healing may not be as effective as it could be.

To summarize, you need to know yourself and be aware of the effects of your environment on your health. Be a health detective. When did you first experience symptoms? Was there a significant stressful event? What is your work history? Where do you live? Are you sensitive to environmental chemicals? Have you been exposed to harmful chemicals? What have you done so far to heal? What's the diagnosis from your physician? What self-care techniques have you used? What is your diet like? Can you describe your lifestyle? Do you have a support system?

Most importantly, do you believe you could be healed? Mark 11:24 states, *...whatever you ask in prayer, believe that you receive it, and you will.* Do you believe nature has the power to heal? What path do you really want to take in life? Do you believe you can reach that goal? Do you have faith in your abilities? Do you believe you could treat yourself at home and heal yourself?

What is your definition of Spirituality? Have you given some thought to exploring your Spirituality? Are you willing to be truthful with everyone involved in your healing process? Are you willing to learn new things and try new ideas and methods to healing? Are you ready to take responsibility for your health? Do you seek out resources and read about your illness? Are you willing to purchase whatever is needed for your wellness?

Do you feel you have the strength and inner resolve to change your thoughts from negative to positive? Do you feel in control of your life? Do you feel you have a strong inner resolve to get well? Do you get discouraged easily? What does it mean to you to live consciously? Do you believe in a higher power? Do you believe there is a world beyond the physical? Do you live a balanced life? Are there situations in your life that cause discomfort? Do you live in the moment, or do you worry about the past or the future?

What is your story? Do you believe in reincarnation? Do you believe in karma? Are you willing to give what it is you need to receive? Do you know how to meditate? Do you exercise regularly? Are you in touch with your purpose in this life? What do you think your obstacles to healing are? Do you want to learn how to heal yourself and others? Do you want to be well?

These are a lifetime of questions I had to ask myself. If you can establish your own truthful answers to these questions, you could be well on your way to healing. Working in complement with your physicians and/or professional counselors, I am willing to be one of the people in your support system.

I am offering my favorite healing modality to you. If you feel you are suffering from any physical, emotional, mental, or spiritual traumas, I would love to help you move forward by conducting three sessions of crystal healing to include:

- *Initiation* – Designed to bring your spirit back to its beginning, and to awaken each center to its own power, unaffected by outside conditionings and beliefs, therefore, allowing for the opening to living with all possibilities.
- *Release* – Designed to let go of any unwanted negative energy, old belief systems, and confusion, allowing new and clear thoughts, feelings, and beliefs to enter.
- *Integration* – Designed to assist in integrating the conflicting feelings, which reside in each of us, achieve a feeling of wholeness and well-being, and aid in clarification of confusing thought patterns and inner turmoil.

I invite you to visit my website at: marilynformella.com for more information.

# Acknowledgements

The people I want to thank are way too numerous to mention individually. First, to those who gave me healing answers freely and without expectation of reciprocity, I am eternally grateful.

I thank all my teachers, friends, and acquaintances in the healing community and to all my clients who trusted me to help you heal.

I wish to thank all my employers and customers who offered me opportunities to shine and who kept me going, especially in times of need.

And, to all the wonderful staff at The Author Incubator. Angela Lauria, you are the angel who encouraged me to tell my story and carry on with a servant's heart. Special thanks to Rae Guyn, who kept me on task and on schedule, and to Heather Mae Russell for being the sweetest author and salesperson on earth.

I also wish to thank all my friends and family who have shown me your kindness and generosity. Special thanks to all my readers, especially those who have the courage to heal.

## About the Author

The author had her first episode with Epstein-Barr Virus at the age of 18 yet wasn't officially diagnosed by her physician until she was 35. She also suffered from the ill effects of Fibromyalgia. Marilyn had unwavering faith that she would someday be healed, and her healing journey was long and hard. Today, at the age of 64, she tells her story about the twists and turns on the road to healing.

Marilyn Formella learned that it is from giving that we receive. She needed healing so she became a healer and learned how to treat herself and her daughter, in addition to people she met along the way. She is self-taught in self-care. Her hope is to bring healing back into the home where it was done more than 50 years ago. The dream is to have community healing/teaching centers all over the world. Hopefully, more and more people will take responsibility for the state of their health by learning how to care for themselves, their loved ones, and others in their communities.

The author worked in the business world in the sales profession. She served as a founding member and President of the National Association for Professional Saleswomen – Milwaukee Chapter. The demands of her profession sent her on a roller coaster ride of ups and downs, experiencing worsening symptoms from Epstein-Barr Virus and Fibromyalgia. Along her healing journey, she learned different healing modalities leading to answers that she is willing to share with others who suffer from the ill effects of these and other chronic illnesses.

Marilyn holds a BA in Business and Management from Alverno College in Milwaukee, WI. She is also a Certified Crystal Healer. The author has experience with other natural healing modalities including: Bach Flower Remedies, Chi Gong, Energy Work using Crystals and Reiki, Essential Oils, Herbology, Homeopathy,

Meditation, Nutrition, Reflexology, and Tai Chi. In addition to the natural healing arts, Marilyn enjoys cooking, exercising, reading, writing, photography, fine art painting, music, and treasure hunting. She is a single mother, having raised a daughter who is now a college instructor.

# Thank You!

I want to sincerely thank you for reading this truthful account spanning over 36 years of my life. It was a trying time for me and, unless you've experienced the debilitating effects of chronic illness, can you truly understand the devastating effects on one's life. I could only hope to be a better writer and express the desperate feelings of impending death during these horrible episodes with the Epstein-Barr Virus. One victim described these episodes as the feeling of "being buried alive."

Allow me to describe one last synchronous event that occurred the evening after I returned home from The Author Incubator, the company in McLean, Virginia that encouraged me to write this book. I woke up in the middle of the night to turn off the TV only to discover an Independent Lens film on PBS about Harvard Ph.D. student, Jennifer Brea, who was stuck down by fever from the Epstein-Barr Virus—*the disease that medicine forgot*. The movie is an award-winning Sundance Film entitled, *Unrest*. Of course, I stayed up to watch it in its entirety and sobbed uncontrollably at the final scene. It was a poignant image of empty shoes belonging to the people who either committed suicide or who died from this illness. I realized I could have been one of them. God bless their souls...may they rest in peace.

# CONTENTS

Chapter One ................................................................. 2
Chapter Two ................................................................. 9
Chapter Three ............................................................. 17
Chapter Four .............................................................. 26
Chapter Five ............................................................... 30
Chapter Six ................................................................ 37
Chapter Seven ............................................................. 42
Chapter Eight ............................................................. 49
Chapter Nine .............................................................. 58
Chapter Ten ............................................................... 64
Chapter Eleven ............................................................ 69
Chapter Twelve ............................................................ 76

*Namaste...the spirit in me honors the spirit in you!*

Made in the USA
San Bernardino, CA
31 March 2019